HurdsHill

A brief history of the family home of Walter Bagehot

Janet Seaton & Barry Winetrobe

FOREWORD

Houses of the famous have a special interest. Lives that affected the world around were lived privately in places often little known to contemporaries who saw the figure on the national or international stage. Walter Bagehot burned bright on the Victorian stage in his short life. His *The English Constitution* has been rediscovered by successive generations of political thinkers while his lively essays on economics and politics are regularly reprinted. In the economic crisis of 2008 it was to Bagehot that western governments turned. His life was made and lived in Langport, born above the bank in the town that was the family business in 1826, connected with the bank all through his life despite his career in London, and he died in 1877 at Hurds Hill, the house that his grandfather had built in the very year of Walter Bagehot's birth, 1826. Hurds Hill was the house he regarded as home, to which he regularly returned. It is for the special historical interest of Walter Bagehot that Hurds Hill is listed Grade II*.

The handsome and unusual colonnaded front dates from after Bagehot's death, probably built for his widow Eliza and her sister Emilie Barrington, but the house that Bagehot knew survives behind, brought back to life after years in institutional use. Standing on Hurds Hill looking over the Somerset Levels the visitor is sharing a view that Walter Bagehot knew and loved, and the compass of his private life is contained in the short distance between here and the churchyard on Langport Hill where he is buried.

Julian Orbach
Architectural historian
Author of the revised edition of *Pevsner's Buildings of England:
South and West Somerset*

CONTENTS

INTRODUCTION

When we were asked by the owners of Hurds Hill, Clifford Lee & David Holmes, to write a brief history of their historic home, we were delighted to accept. As Janet chairs the Langport & District History Society, and Barry chairs the Bagehot Memorial Fund, this was an opportunity to learn more about the family home of the Bagehots, and to commemorate one of the Langport area's most important sites. We hope that everyone who reads this booklet will find it interesting and informative.

We thank the following for their help and support on this project: David and Clifford; Julian Orbach; Jo Stradling; Maude Musgrove; Somerset Heritage Centre; the Ruddle family; Pamela McKee and David Wyatt in Australia, and all the others who responded to our request for memories of, and material about, Hurds Hill.

Every effort has been made to source all images used, and to seek the appropriate permissions, but if we have accidently breached copyright, we will happily rectify the oversight in future editions. We also welcome feedback, especially any corrections, additional information or images.

Walter Bagehot and the Bagehots of Langport

This is not the story of the Bagehots, but, to understand Hurds Hill and its place in Langport life, a very brief history of Walter Bagehot and his family is appropriate.

Walter Bagehot (1826-1877) was a famous Victorian banker and writer on economic and constitutional matters, who remains influential to this day. Born in 1826 in Langport, he was the son of Thomas Watson Bagehot, a senior director of Stuckey's Bank, a major regional banking house, and Edith, a member of the Stuckey family and sister of the important banker, Vincent Stuckey of Hill House, Langport. The two families dominated Langport commerce, especially through the Stuckey & Bagehot trading company based by the River Parrett (at what is now Great Bow Wharf) for over a

WALTER BAGEHOT

A LANGPORT MAN

AN INTERNATIONAL FIGURE

> *"The great pleasure in life is doing what people say you cannot do"*
> *Walter Bagehot, 1853*

WHO WAS WALTER BAGEHOT?

Walter Bagehot (1826-1877) was a famous Victorian banker and writer on economic and constitutional matters.

He was born on 3 February 1826 in Bank House in Cheapside, Langport. His father, Thomas, was an active partner in Stuckey's Bank, a powerful regional bank. His mother Edith came from the Stuckey family, who, with the Bagehots, were the major commercial force in Langport in the 19th century.

Bagehot was educated in Langport, Bristol and at University College London. He helped run Stuckey's Bank, and also wrote books and articles on a wide variety of subjects. His two most important works have remained standard texts in their respective fields: *The English constitution* (1867) and *Lombard Street* (1873).

He was the editor of *The Economist* from 1861 until his death. He was consulted by leading figures such as Gladstone, and was much admired by US President, Woodrow Wilson, who made a pilgrimage to Bagehot's grave in 1896 and again in 1899.

In 1858, Bagehot married Eliza Wilson, eldest daughter of James Wilson MP, the founder of *The Economist*. They had no children. Bagehot died in the Langport family home at Herd's Hill in 1877 and was buried in All Saints' Church.

His family home, now known as Hurds Hill, is a Business School (www.hurdshill.com) and is not open to the public.

****

BAGEHOT MEMORIAL FUND

In 2011 the Bagehot Memorial Fund was set up to commemorate Walter Bagehot in Langport and beyond. It maintains Bagehot's grave, installed the Town Garden interpretation board, and organizes talks, exhibitions of 'Bagehotiana' and an annual Bagehot Debate. It operates a website on 'all things Bagehot', a Twitter feed and Facebook page. For more information on the Bagehot Memorial Fund:

- Website: www.bagehotlangport.co.uk
- Facebook: Bagehot Memorial Fund
- Twitter: @bagehotlangport
- Email: Clerk@langport-tc.gov.uk (financial); Bagehot@seatrobe.co.uk (other)

****

STILL RELEVANT TODAY

Bagehot's views, especially on the constitution, the monarchy, banking and finance, remain influential. Virtually every day he is mentioned somewhere in the media and academic circles around the world.

The historian GM Young described Bagehot in 1948 as 'the greatest Victorian'. In 1967, unveiling a Blue Plaque to Bagehot in London, the then Prime Minister Harold Wilson said: "Bagehot towered over the world of journalism and public affairs during his lifetime, and was the most acute observer of the political and economic society in which he lived."

In 1986, another PM, Margaret Thatcher, described Bagehot as "perhaps the most distinguished of all financial journalists. His work illumined not only the problems of his time, but our time ... I have no doubt that 100 years from now it will still be read."

Around the world there are many things, including academic fellowships and prestigious prizes and lectures, named in Bagehot's honour. In 2009 The Royal Mint produced a commemorative £5 silver coin in its London Olympics series which featured a Bagehot quote: 'Nations touch at their summits'.

There is even an asteroid, discovered in 1973, called *2901 Bagehot*!

Unlike many of his Victorian contemporaries, he wrote in a lively, quotable style. He described Parliament as "nothing less than a big meeting of more or less idle people" and observed that a "royal family sweetens politics by the seasonable addition of nice and pretty events." On banking crises, he declared that "the cause of panic is the expectation of insolvency."

About literature, he said that "the reason why so few good books are written is that so few people that can write know anything." He thought that Dickens "describes London like a special correspondent for posterity."

****

WHERE CAN I SEE MORE?

Here are the main Bagehot sites in Langport. More information is available on the Bagehot website: www.bagehotlangport.co.uk.

There is a stone plaque on his birthplace, Bank House, in Cheapside, installed in 1916.

In All Saints' Church on The Hill, the splendid West Window was installed by Bagehot's widow in his memory. You can also visit his gravesite, a listed monument, in the south east corner of the churchyard.

Just behind Langport Town Hall is the Walter Bagehot Town Garden, where an illustrated interpretation board was erected in 2013, providing information on Bagehot's life, work and legacy.

century. Bagehot helped run the banking business, and also wrote on a wide variety of subjects. His two most important works remain classics: *The English constitution* (1867) and *Lombard Street* (1873). He edited *The Economist* from 1861 until his death, and was consulted by leading figures including Gladstone. Future US President Woodrow Wilson was a great fan of Bagehot's works and made a pilgrimage to Bagehot's grave in 1896 and 1899. In 1858, Bagehot married Eliza, eldest daughter of James Wilson MP, founder of *The Economist*. They had no children. Bagehot died in 1877 at Hurds Hill, and was buried in All Saints' Churchyard on Langport Hill.

Walter Bagehot (1826-1877)

Herd's vs Hurds

There have been several spellings of the names of both the house and the hill on which it stands, mainly variants of Herds/Hurds Hill, with and without an apostrophe. During the Bagehot period, c1820s-1930s, the location and the house were both generally known as Herd's Hill. For convenience, we will use the modern 'Hurds Hill', except where the context requires otherwise, as in direct quotations.

CHAPTER 1

HURDS HILL IN ITS SETTING

Early history

The hill upon which the modern Hurds Hill house stands owed its historical importance to the local geography of the area. It looms over a strategic river crossing of the River Parrett (now the Bow Bridge) which for centuries operated as a natural border between different tribes or communities. This was especially so in ancient times when more of modern 'Somerset' remained under water for some or all of the year. With Langport Hill (now The Hill) on the east side, Hurds Hill on the west side was a natural defensive position for a frontier settlement.

There are brief references to finds and traces from the prehistoric and later periods on Hurds Hill. There is also evidence of Roman occupation in the vicinity, including the site of a possible villa, and the discovery of a burial site in 1836 and of coins in 1867. With the river crossing, there was probably a rudimentary Roman road from Bow Street in Langport to the east and past Hurds Hill to the west.

Both in the pre- and post-Roman periods, the two hills would have been occupied by warring tribes, with the River Parrett as an obvious frontier demarcation. These were often indigenous tribes standing against the various waves of continental invaders, such as the Dumnonii Britons on Hurds Hill and the Belgae on Langport Hill, and later the Britons on Hurds Hill and the Saxons on Langport Hill.

Hurds Hill sits in an area steeped in early British history. Arthur himself is said to have commanded the troops at the battle of Longborth, which may be Langport. Arthur's Avalon was of course at Glastonbury. The Somerset Levels are where King Alfred sheltered from the Danish onslaught in the ninth century, hiding and re-arming on the Isle of Athelney before emerging to defeat the Danes at Edington in 878. It was at Aller just north of Hurds

3

Hill that Guthrum, the Danish leader, was baptised Christian after Alfred's victory.

On the Hill, west of the present house, sat the St. Mary Magdalene Leper Hospital, which was founded around 1280. By the early 14th century it was an almshouse, which lasted until the mid-1500s. East of the house there was a church for Westover, mentioned as early as 1401. Substantial medieval settlements grew below the hill at Southwick (Frog Lane) and Langport Westover.

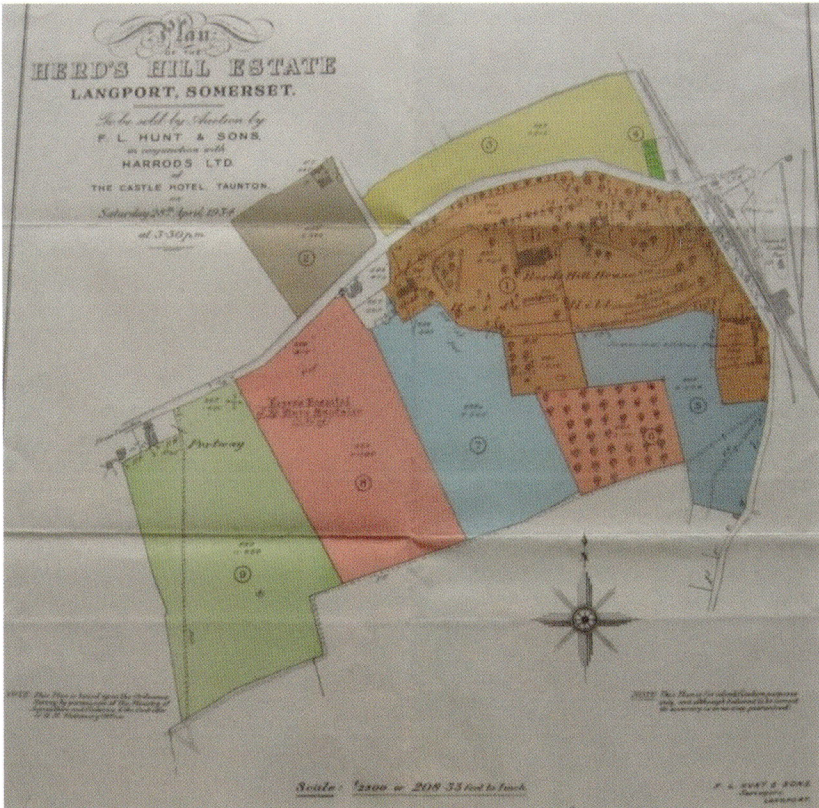

Map of the estate in 1934

After the Norman Conquest, the surrounding area would have been 'owned' by local lords, such as the Rivels from about 1160; the de Lortys from the early 13th century (Henry de Lorty, grandson of the original lord, was buried in Curry Rivel Church); the de Montacutes from the later 14th century until the fall of Richard II, and then the Beauforts.

There is a rather fanciful story that, at the English Civil War Battle of Langport on 10 July 1645, a famous eye-witness to the campaign, Richard Baxter, a chaplain in the Roundhead Army, actually stood on Hurds Hill with the victorious commander, Sir Thomas Fairfax, and viewed the desperate Royalist retreat through Langport.

The Bagehot era

The modern history of Hurds Hill reflects the huge social and economic changes since the 18th century, especially the growth of new forms of communication and trade. From it, one could see the turnpike road through Westover in the 1750s; improved river navigation and commerce (and a new Bow Bridge) promoted by the Parrett Navigation Company in the 1830s-40s (supported by the important local commercial businesses run by the two intertwined families of Stuckey and Bagehot, with its wharves and warehouses adjacent to the Bridge, and, in 1853, the coming of the railway, with a station at Langport Westover.

In the era of enclosures and the accumulation of small plots into larger farms and estates, the Stuckey and Bagehot families gradually bought up the land (much of it church land) on and around Hurds Hill. Contemporary records show that even in 1820 the site of the present house was still arable land. In 1826-7, Robert and Mary Bagehot, grandparents of Walter Bagehot, built Hurds Hill house, and the Bagehot era began.

Walter Bagehot was born on 3 February 1826 in Bank House (now Bank Chambers) in Cheapside, Langport, where his father, Thomas, managed Stuckey's Bank. When Robert Bagehot died in 1836, Thomas inherited Hurds Hill, and the family moved up there. Both Walter's parents remained there until first Edith died there in 1870, and Thomas in 1881.

Walter himself, as a student, banker and journalist, and after his marriage in 1858 to Eliza Wilson, lived in many different properties, especially in London, over his lifetime. However, he always spent large periods of time at Hurds Hill, such as when he abandoned a proposed law career in London in 1852 to work in the family's Langport Bank and to be with his ill mother.

Walter died at the young age of 51 on 24 March 1877, and his widow (they had no children) continued to live part of the year at Hurds Hill and the rest in London with her Wilson family and their wide social circle. On Thomas Bagehot's death in 1881, Eliza inherited the house, and spent much time and effort improving it. In this she was assisted by her sister, Emilie, who had married Russell Barrington in 1868, and who gradually came to exert a strong influence over Eliza, especially at Hurds Hill, which became a frequent haunt of the various members of the Wilson clan.

When Eliza died in 1921, aged 89, Emilie Barrington and her son Guy lived on in Hurds Hill, under the terms of Eliza's will. The Bagehot link ended on her death in 1933, and the house and its land were sold off, thus breaking up the single Bagehot estate of around 65 acres.

Later owners and uses

The house and the wider estate passed through various owners, the first being Brigadier Henry Courtenay Hawtrey (1882-1961), who was for several years until his retirement in 1934, Aide-de-camp to King George V, and who won the gold medal for the 5 mile run at the 1906 Athens Olympics.

Mr & Mrs Lavington Evans lived in the house from the late 1930s to the 1950s. Mr Evans had served in the Indian Civil Service, and his wife took an active part in local community activities.

The house had undergone much alteration by the time it was sold at auction in 1970 following the financial demise of its rather colourful owner at the time, the Russian émigré businessman Alexander Ilytch Shenkman. He came to Hurds Hill in about 1964. One of his plans was to turn the station buildings at Langport West (which had just closed) into stables for polo ponies. He had interests in the steel industry, and served at one time as Chairman of the Association of Iron and Steel Exporters and Importers, but he got into financial difficulties in the late 1960s and was forced to liquidate some of his assets, including Hurds Hill. His death notice in the *Times* of 25 February 2004 said, "Alexander Ilytch 'Sasha' aged 80, died peacefully in his sleep on Saturday 21st February, after a full and interesting life. ... He was much loved and will be enormously missed."

Herd's Hill House
Langport
Somerset

Sale catalogues from 1934 and 1970

In 1970 the house and grounds comprised around 30 acres. It was bought by the Ruddle family from Somerton, who lived here for over 10 years. Kim Ruddle was married from the house in 1972, and caused much amusement by arriving at the church in the bucket of a digger, since her father was a builder.

When it was sold again in the early 1980s, to be operated as a residential care home for around 30 residents, the estate connected to the house was only 7 acres.

The present owners bought the house and grounds, now about 4 acres, in 2011, and, after extensive renovation, have returned it to a private house, and added a business school. On and around the Hill itself are various houses and other properties not connected with the current Hurds Hill estate.

Bagehot's chroniclers at Hurds Hill

Emilie Barrington (known publicly as Mrs Russell Barrington) was not only Walter Bagehot's sister-in-law and long-time resident of Hurds Hill until her death in 1933, but was also Walter's biographer and editor of his works.

Bagehot's most recent chronicler was Norman St.John Stevas (1929-2012), later Lord St John of Fawsley, a Conservative MP, and cabinet minister under Margaret Thatcher,. His 15-volume *Collected Works* was begun in 1959 and completed in 1986) He visited Langport several times from 1957, where he met people connected with the Bagehots, and worked at Hurds Hill, as can be seen in this photo of 6 August 1967, showing him correcting proofs:

He also collected Bagehot-related items (which he called Bagehotiana), such as candlesticks, Walter's travelling briefcase and his degree certificates, which he exhibited at *The Economist* in 1966.

Hurds Hill in Australia

In the Coromandel Valley, just outside Adelaide, South Australia is a home called Hurd's Hill. It was built in 1849 for the family of Thomas and Harriet Matthews, who came from Pitney in Somerset (about 4 miles east of Hurds Hill). It is sometimes said to have been named after a 'Hurds Hill' in Somerset, although it is more likely that its name reflects Harriet Matthews' Hurd family.

The Australian Hurd's Hill is regarded as an historic house and is the subject of a recently published book by its current owner.

Hurd's Hill, South Australia

CHAPTER 2

FEATURES OF THE HOUSE

Hurds Hill was built by Robert Bagehot, Walter Bagehot's grandfather. He and his wife Mary found the damp atmosphere of Langport unhealthy and, by January 1825, had selected a hill site for their new home. Following the commissioning of plans from local architects, based on suggestions by Walter's father, Thomas, an architect from Bridgwater called Carver was chosen, though his original grand designs were somewhat modified. Work was begun in February 1826, a few days after Walter's birth, and he was brought as a babe in arms to the laying of the foundation stone.

Building progressed slowly, but by 1 August 1827, Mary Bagehot wrote: "Our house is nearly finished, but there are some of the niceties about which I would willingly superintend but not having my own carpenter, in many things I fear I shall fail, for they do not put up houses in the country with the attention to comfort they do in large towns, we are now having it painted and the court and offices are being paved, the garden is about to be formed." By November, Robert and Mary Bagehot had moved in.

Hurds Hill is a substantial Regency villa. The only image of it before the late Victorian alterations shows a stuccoed villa of some distinction with a porch of paired square columns and blind arches over the ground floor windows on each side. Giant panelled piers emphasise the outer angles and a cornice carries the eaves of the hipped roof. All these features can still be seen on the side of the house.

The front was embellished probably after the death of Walter's father Thomas in 1881 for Walter's widow Eliza and her sister Emilie, but the date of this work cannot yet be pinpointed. What was done was an unusual rather 'American' refronting with a two-storey colonnade repeating the square piers of the original porch, all done in Ham stone. The piers are continuous on the upper floor, but on the ground floor the outer bays are solid, with triple sash windows lighting the two main front rooms. It is a subtle composition, the outer parts slightly stepped forward and with pediments, the first-floor colonnade giving strong effects of light and shade in sunlight. Probably at the same time the principal entrance was moved to the north side, with a new Ham stone porch set to the left of the original north façade, which remains as in 1826.

An early view of Hurds Hill, before Eliza embellished it

The interior of the house has changed over the years but the bones of the original plan are still apparent. This would have had a dining-room and drawing-room on each side of an entrance hall facing west, and the staircase behind, probably in line with the front door. The chief features of interest are two fine marble chimneypieces of the early 19th century , but it cannot be said if they are original to the house. The late 19th century alteration made a new entrance hall at the north east and the staircase was remodelled probably in the early 20th century.

In the south east room is the most interesting reminder of Walter Bagehot. Here is a deep inglenook fireplace such as were becoming fashionable in the 1870s just before Bagehot died. A long beam on stone columns shelters a charming recess with a fireplace. What sadly has gone is the decoration in

11

wonderfully rich painted tiles of Islamic colours by William de Morgan, the leading ceramicist of the day (and the son of one of Walter's former professors at UCL, Augustus de Morgan). There was a giant panel of a galleon under sail over the fireplace and luscious floral tiles each side. The tiles at lower level each side of the fireplace seem to have had the copper-lustre fishes for which de Morgan was famous.

De Morgan tiles in the sitting room inglenook fireplace

Emilie, who seemed to be particularly adept at spending Bagehot money, encouraged Walter and Eliza to patronise both Morris and de Morgan when they were furnishing and refurbishing their properties in London and Langport. Walter wrote to her about the redecoration of their London house: "the great man himself, William Morris, is composing the drawing room, as he would an ode." In her biography of Walter Emilie gleefully described how he "would at times meet William Morris at the Bloomsbury depot when choosing papers and tiles, and the two would talk poetry as well as furniture."

She thought such artistic tastes too radical for Somerset of the 1870s:

> The moral severity with which these prophets treated decoration and all matters of taste was not at that time quite understood in the rural districts of Somerset. The few smart houses near Herd's Hill were still decorated by second-hand French designs and white and gilt ornament. Relations and neighbours were puzzled by Walter's choice. They were inclined to think Morris papers and furniture too plain and "rather queer".

In 1934, when Emilie's death severed the last link with the Bagehot family, the furniture was auctioned off separately from the buildings. This advertisement gives a flavour of the quality and quantity of the contents:

BY DIRECTION OF THE EXECUTORS OF MRS. RUSSELL BARRINGTON, AND ALSO OF THE TRUSTEE OF MRS. WALTER BAGEHOT, DECEASED.

HERD'S HILL, LANGPORT.

SALE of the VALUABLE ANTIQUE and OTHER HOUSEHOLD FURNITURE, comprising:—Charles II., Queen Anne, Chippendale and Sheraton Chairs; 2 Antique Long Case Clocks; 10 Oak Bible Boxes; Fine Chippendale Mahogany Arm-chair, with carved arms and legs; Indo-Persian Inlaid Ivory Desk; Fine Louis XVI. Inlaid Cherrywood Writing Table; Antique Cedarwood and other Chests; Chippendale Mahogany and other Gate-leg Tables; 8-day Bracket Clock; "Steck" Pianola Piano, in mahogany case; Empire Inlaid Mahogany Break-front Sideboard; Set of 9 Hepplewhite Mahogany Dining Chairs; Charles II. Walnut Seat; Sheraton Mahogany Dining Table, 9ft. 9in. long; 2 Jacobean Carved Oak Refectory Tables; Pair Inlaid Mahogany Hepplewhite Card Tables, on cluster legs; 2 Georgian Mahogany Wing Arm-chairs; Bedsteads and Bedding; Tapestry and other Curtains; Blankets and Linen; China; Silver; Plate; Glass, &c.

The LIBRARY, comprising about 4,000 Vols.; also numerous Outside Effects, in all over 1,000 Lots.

MESSRS. F. L. HUNT & SONS have been favoured with instructions to SELL the above by AUCTION on WEDNESDAY, THURSDAY and FRIDAY, 11th, 12th and 13th APRIL, 1934, commencing at 11.30 a.m. precisely each Day.

Catalogues price 6d. Separate Book Catalogue free on request.   [10400

Western Gazette, 23 Mar 1934, p.1

The interior of the house has also been the subject of several paintings by Nina Stewart, a distant relative.

*View looking east towards the main staircase
by Nina Stewart, c.1920s*

Today the house has been tastefully restored to much of its former glory, although it is sad that so little trace of its famous inhabitants – and their decorations – remains.

Walter Bagehot's parents, Thomas Watson Bagehot and Edith Bagehot

Walter's wife, Eliza and her sister Emilie Barrington

CHAPTER 3

HOME LIFE

The Hurds Hill estate has always housed either private residences or commercial or agricultural businesses. Therefore it is understandable that virtually all the documentary evidence of life there over nearly two centuries derives from the era of its occupation by the Bagehot family.

The Bagehots loved Hurds Hill. According to Emilie Barrington's biography of Walter, "Herd's Hill, their home, was worshipped by Walter as a boy. Countless letters exist … showing the romantic love they all felt for this Herd's Hill." In one letter to Walter, then a student at Bristol College, his father Thomas wrote "you may picture us to yourself, wandering about at Herd's Hill, still admiring its bright mornings and serene and beautiful moonlight nights, although having lost in you one of its greatest charms."

Later when he moved to London to study at UCL, Walter showed signs of home-sickness, when he wrote to his mother in October 1842, "I must confess to having felt rather dismal .. when I think of Herd's Hill and you all sitting quietly and happily down amid all its beauties, while I am toiling here in the midst of dust and smoke."

Emilie herself fell in love with Hurds Hill from her first visit on 23 July 1858, calling it "the place which has meant home to me more than any other place in the world for many years past":

> On arriving at Herd's Hill it was as if one had stepped back into the world of a hundred years ago, a world of Jane Austen's novels. A delightful world it was. No place ever possessed a stronger character of its own. It seemed set fixed in its own little frame, so fixed that there was little need of formality.

However, there seemed always to be a darker side to family life at Hurds Hill, often relating to physical and mental illness. As well as Walter's frequent illnesses, and his premature death in 1877 aged only 51, two of his mother's children by her first marriage had died young and the other was mentally ill, and Walter's brother, Watson, had died aged three. These tragedies affected Edith severely, and she spent some time in an asylum in Bristol, which was a constant worry to her devoted family. Later, Emilie's son, Guy, also suffered throughout his life from mental difficulties.

Because of Hurds Hill's relatively isolated location, these troubles could largely be hidden from the outside world. But it imposed severe strains on the family, especially the young Walter. Despite this, Emilie noted that, in Walter's childhood, "with all its trials and 'dark realities', the home life at Herd's Hill was a beautiful life."

Walter's parents were Christians, though of different denominations, which made his childhood Sundays busy. He attended his father's Unitarian services in the morning in the drawing room, and in the afternoon he went with his Anglican mother, Edith, to the local parish churches at Langport, Huish Episcopi, or Curry Rivel. Emilie recalled Edith's casual proselytising: "On the first morning of our visit, after Mr. Bagehot and Walter had left the breakfast table, Mrs. Bagehot, as was her custom, began reading the Psalms while the butler cleared away the breakfast, explaining to us that by this means she insured his getting some Bible reading every day."

The dining room in the 1970s

During the working lives of Thomas and his son Walter they would have been regulars in Langport, as they made their way down to the Stuckey's Bank in Cheapside. Local lore relates that Watson (as he was known) was so punctual each morning in his perambulation from Hurds Hill to the Bank "that clocks were regulated by his passing and the local phrase became: 'Tis such-and-such a time by Mr Watson.'"

Sitting atop a hill, the estate was spared direct attack from the flooding common on the Somerset Levels, though the residents' lives would have been affected by its impact on the surrounding area. In November 1894, it was reported that among the food supplies distributed to the poorer citizens was "a quantity of hot coffee" from Mrs Bagehot.

Hurds Hill's lofty position left it very exposed to gales and storms. In December 1872, according to Eliza Bagehot's diary there was a "dreadful gale evening – 7 trees blown down at Herd's Hill." Nearly a decade later, another gale demolished, according to the local paper, "a large number of nests at the Rookery, on Herd's Hill; and the trees in the orchards and gardens were considerably damaged."

The local press also reported the improvements in local amenities and transport over the years. In November 1883, a vestry meeting discussed a proposed new road "so as to avoid the steep gradient now existing at Herd's Hill." Fifteen years later, in May 1899, when the financing of an improved water supply by Langport Rural District Council (which administered a much larger area than the present Town Council) to Curry Rivel and Drayton was the subject of a public inquiry, Russell Barrington was in attendance on behalf of the Hurds Hill estate, and, in the words of a press report, "asked that the supply might be taken a half-mile further to Herd's Hill."

Social life

The Bagehots were part of Victorian society, especially in London, mixing with the country's social, artistic and political elite, some of whom would come to visit Hurds Hill. Even as late as July 1931, Emilie Barrington was inviting the poet and writer Siegfried Sassoon to her Somerset retreat, though it is not known if he accepted.

The family were active in the local community, lending their name to various worthy causes in typical Victorian manner. At New Year 1882, for example, around 100 senior citizens of the community were each given sixpence from the estate of the recently deceased Thomas Bagehot.

They would often make the house and grounds available for events and activities. These included a summer's afternoon party for 150 children from the Congregational Chapel Sunday School in a field on Hurds Hill in August 1887; military drilling by the local Company of Volunteers in the grounds in July 1891; a lecture on 'Poor Law administration: past and present' by a George H Leonard in October 1904, followed by a discussion, and a luncheon provided by Eliza; and a drawing room meeting of the Police Court Mission of the Church of England Temperance Society in September 1908.

Emilie encouraged Eliza, in the words of one later commentator, "to bring a bit of Kensington culture to the local Langport inhabitants" by arranging for a series of four weekly lectures one September in the early 1900s on topics ranging from Samuel Johnson to Rudyard Kipling's poetry. Eliza, perhaps rather reluctantly, also opened Hurds Hill's gardens and grounds to the public on Sunday afternoons each summer, who came in large numbers to visit "these charming grounds." In July 1908, the Town Band gave a concert in the grounds "to the delight of a large number of promenaders."

Hurds Hill's current owners have continued this tradition by making it available to the local community. In particular, they have hosted a number of events relating to the Bagehots, run by the Bagehot Memorial Fund or by the Langport and District History Society. All these activities have been very popular, and have given local people a rare opportunity in the nearly two hundred years of Hurds Hill to see inside the house itself and its grounds.

An exhibition of Bagehotiana in the dining room at Hurds Hill in 2013

CHAPTER 4

RUNNING THE HOUSE

The number of servants in a Victorian household was an indicator of the wealth of the family as well as a necessary way of managing a large estate. Some of them lived in, and their names are recorded on the census, but there were many others who would have lived nearby.

Census records regularly list four staff living on the premises until the death of Thomas Watson Bagehot, Walter's father, in 1881. One was generally a man - probably a manservant or a butler, and there were three women - one older, who was probably a cook and/or housekeeper, and two younger women, who would have done the more menial tasks such as blacking the grates, polishing the silver and preparing the vegetables. After that the household became smaller, as Eliza, Walter's widow, spent most of her time in London. This group of 13 staff were photographed in about 1900, probably when the house was fully occupied.

It was prudent to provide good working and living conditions for their valued staff. The particulars for the sale of the house in 1934 detailed the servants' accommodation: 'The domestic offices comprise: staff sitting room, kitchen, scullery (h. and c.) with independent boiler, pantry (h. and c.), 2 larders, box room, maids' WC and good cellarage below…. Six comfortable bedrooms for servants, each having a fireplace.'

From time to time the residents of Hurds Hill would have had to advertise for staff. One of the post-Bagehot owners, Mrs Lavington Evans, placed ads in the local papers, promising applicants 'good outings' (1938) or 'good wages and every consideration' (1950).

COOK Wanted. Three maids kept. Sitting-room, own bedroom. Good outings. Modern conveniences, electric light.—Apply Mrs. Evans, Herds Hill, Langport. [12106

Western Gazette, 14 Oct 1938 p.8

COOK and Parlourman, or Cook and Parlourmaid. Wanted for country house. Very comfortable conditions, all modern conveniences, on bus route, near shops. Good wages and every consideration.—Write Mrs. Lavington-Evans, Herds Hill, Langport, Somerset. [65507

Western Gazette, 27 Oct 1950 p.4

Some adverts, like this from 1915, were plainer:

WANTED, STRONG LAD, about 16 or 17, for housework, under parlourmaid, and to go with carriage; wages £18 and livery.— Mrs. Russell Barrington, Herds Hill, Langport.

Devon and Exeter Gazette, 17 Dec 1915, p.4

Less than two years later, in a tragic incident, the family's coachman committed suicide. Eliza's diary gives a clue as to the reason:

Wednesday 12 September 1917
Valentine locked himself into coach house during morning & was not found till the carriage was wanted, he had been suffering dreadfully from neuritis, & he hanged himself when alone. Dr. was sent for & his wife slept here, after attending to the last sad rites at their cottage, telegraphing to her sister, & his.

It's sobering to think that this photograph of Russell Barrington's carriage may depict the unfortunate George Valentine.

When Russell Barrington died, his coffin was carried into the church at Curry Rivel by six gardeners and estate workmen from Hurds Hill, three of whom were members of the Stacey family.

In the Victorian era some servants stayed with the family for many years, particularly the live-in ones, whom employers preferred to be unmarried. Ann Millard, a local woman, lived at Hurds Hill for over twenty years. Eliza made a brief note in her diary on Saturday 20 October 1867: 'Poor old Ann Millard died'. Others, however, clearly inspired much greater affection.

Susan Speechley, usually referred to as 'Spee', is said to have been with the family for more than 50 years. She was certainly living as a housekeeper with Walter and Eliza in the early years of their marriage, and remained with the family long after Walter's death. When she was dying they brought her to Hurds Hill, as Eliza's diary relates:

Tuesday 28 July 1885
We all with Mrs Speechley left Paddington at 1.45 and had a saloon carriage on her account, not changing all the way. Guy and Mr Suckling met us at Langport Station at 8.

The end came on 17th August. Eliza wrote:

Upstairs with headache. Sat with Spee morning. She was very ill all day and died suddenly without pain at 9 – soon after Mr Brooke's last visit when the nurses were getting her to bed. I was called and sent for Emilie. We & Ethel stayed until the doctor cd. be brought.' The next day she continued: 'Emilie & I drove to Curry morning – Mr Mules absent, but Mrs Mules took us round churchyard & we chose a pretty spot for Spee's grave.

Mrs Maude Musgrove (née Parsons) still today remembers her mother in the 1920s entertaining the cooks from the Hurds Hill and Burton Pynsent estates to Sunday lunch if they had the day off, to give them a break from their own cooking duties.

CHAPTER 5

THE GROUNDS

When Thomas Watson Bagehot, Walter's father, moved from Bank Chambers to Hurds Hill in 1836, it is said that he took his mulberry tree with him, and the garden still has a mulberry tree, though possibly not the same one. He was obviously interested in the gardens, as Walter's sister-in-law Emilie Barrington observed of Thomas in her biography of Walter:

> He was a great lover of beauty in Nature. He planted and laid out the grounds of Herd's Hill with the eye of an artist, securing delightful vistas through the trees of the churches of Langport and Huish Episcopi and of the distant moorlands and hills.

Thomas was one of the earliest customers of the famous Kelways Nurseries, which was founded in Langport in 1851. In July of that year he was stocking up on soft fruit (rather late in the season), as this bill for strawberries, redcurrants, raspberries and gooseberries reveals:

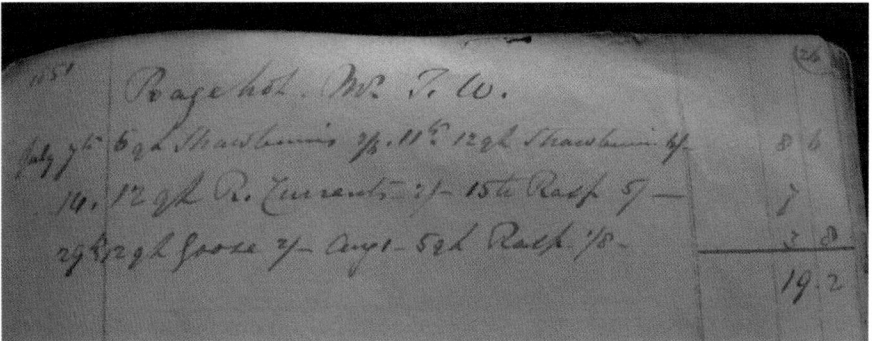

Twenty years later, strawberries were still being well cared for. The *Western Gazette* of 5 July 1872 records that "Mr W Case, gardener to T. W. Bagehot Esq., of Herd's Hill, has recently gathered several strawberries measuring six inches in circumference, and weighing nearly two ounces each."

Eliza, Walter's widow, loved the gardens and took a keen interest in their development. An entry in her diary for 3 August 1885 records, "Spent morning out with R. Halsey, Pittard and Case, settling sites for ponds, and how to take road across old one."

William Case, who was born in Huish Episcopi in about 1820, describes himself as the Head Gardener in the 1871 census and probably worked there for over 20 years. In 1881 he was living in the Gardener's House. He died in 1889 and is buried in St Mary's, Huish Episcopi.

This photo of the gardening staff is thought to date from about 1890. Mr Davidge is in the middle, and Tom Stacey, on the left, is described as Head Gardener, so perhaps he had taken over from William.

As was common at the time, the owners of large gardens would enter their flowers and produce in the local horticultural shows. Hurds Hill entries were regular winners. At the 1881 Taunton Flower Show, for example, Eliza Bagehot won first prizes for a melon, a dish of 6 peaches grown in the open air, and a dish of 6 nectarines grown under glass. An advertisement in 1923 lists the estate as having a vinery, a peach house and four other glasshouses.

Walter Bagehot spent much of his childhood at Hurds Hill, and made full use of the gardens. At the age of three he used to charge around the gardens on a hobby horse called 'Jockey Poney'. Emilie Barrington said that he "lived much in his imagination", and used a toy sword to devastating effect in the flowerbeds. "He would use it at Herd's Hill to lash off the heads of flowers with terrible force, imagining himself the leader of hosts and the demolisher of thousands and ten thousands of the Saracens." In later life, when he came back to Langport to look after his mother, he had a set of steps cut into the north-east corner of the grounds so that he could get to the station at the bottom of the hill more quickly to catch his train. They can still be seen at the corner where Frog Lane meets the main road.

Visitors were as impressed with the gardens as they were with the house. Sir Mountstuart Grant Duff, a former Minister and family friend, wrote in his diary for 5 July 1892:

> Returned to London yesterday afternoon from Herd's Hill, whither I went with Mrs. Greg on the 30th ult. The place was looking lovely, the rose garden in perfection, the two great trees of Portugal laurel, on the sloping lawn, covered with their white flowers, the distances singularly clear and blue though no rain fell, and the weather perfection.

When the estate was sold in 1934, after Emilie's death, it comprised 65 acres, of which the grounds of the house itself amounted to just over 16 acres. The sale particulars gave further details:

> The gardens and grounds have an exceptional charm, and are studded with elm trees of enormous size and other fine specimen forest and ornamental trees. Sloping lawns and terraces with balustrades of Ham stone lead to a large rose garden and bowling green, backed by a high yew hedge, beyond which there are further gardens and a lily pond. In addition there is a walled-in kitchen garden of about 1½ acres, with Gardener's House and range of glasshouses adjoining, also the stone built and thatched small Farm House, together with a semi-detached Cottage.

The rose garden was pictured in the brochure, and a comparison with later views shows how it gradually lost its glory, and was eventually removed in the 1980s as requiring too much maintenance.

The gardens in 1934

The same view in the 1980s

This aerial photo was taken in the 1980s. A faint outline can be seen, showing where the rose beds were, but they had been grassed over. To the right a small white square indicates a clay pigeon shoot enclosure. This view also shows the swimming pool under construction.

The glasshouses at the bottom of the picture were let out separately in the 1920s as a part of a market garden business. After the break-up of the estate in the 1930s, this area was cultivated as a nursery which later became Portway Nurseries.

LAST WORD

We conclude this account of Hurds Hill with an evocative description from the conclusion of Emilie Barrington's 1915 biography of Walter Bagehot, when, following his early death in 1877, his family continued to live there:

> Happily for some of these few, albeit their sun is nearing the horizon, his home is still their home, the Herds Hill, so beloved by his parents and by him from his childhood. There it is, ever recalling to memory that vivid life associated with them. There are the walks, the lawns from which his father opened vistas through the branches of the elm trees to further beauties beyond; to a sight of that little river Parret a blue ribbon winding amidst the damp of green moorland meadows; to the view of the church towers, aged, noble sentinels, rising steadfast amidst a vaporous landscape. There still is the steep pathway, the short cut that Walter would shoot down in all haste to catch his train, a lovely pathway branched over by the big arbutus tree, brilliant in winter with crimson strawberries and white bell-flowers, and by the wide spreading lime-tree, bright yellow-green, and the copper beech, cornelian scarlet in the spring, purple crimson in the summer, their trunks buttressed against a steep bank of primroses and moss; the views over the moors to the Quantock and Mendip Hills; to the mound in the moors marking the place where Alfred the Great burnt the famous cakes. All these things still are there as we wander on those lawns; and round us still hover living associations with those three to whom they were so dear.

A watercolour painting of the gardens, by Nina Stewart

FURTHER READING

Emilie Barrington. *Works and Life of Walter Bagehot*, 10 vols, 1915

Norman St John-Stevas, *The collected works of Walter Bagehot*, 15 vols, 1986

Norman St. John-Stevas. *Walter Bagehot: a study of his life and thought*, 1959

David Melville Ross, *Langport and its church*, 1911

Martha Westwater. *The Wilson sisters: a biographical study of upper middle-class Victorian Life*, 1984

See also:

Walter Bagehot & Bagehot Memorial Fund: www.bagehotlangport.co.uk

Langport & District History Society:
https://sites.google.com/site/langportheritage

ILLUSTRATIONS

We acknowledge, with grateful thanks, the permission of the following to reproduce their images:
David Holmes & Clifford Lee (front cover); the Bagehot Memorial Fund (pages 4,7,8,11,12,14,15,30); the Ruddle family (pages 17,20,28,29); Langport & District History Society (pages 21,23,26), Pamela McKee (page 9) and Charles Lloyd (page 25).

HurdsHill

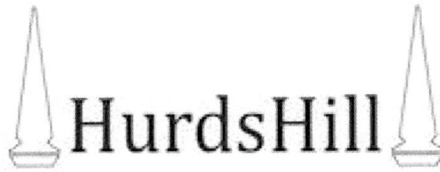

Business School &
Meeting Rooms
Residential or Day Hire

Whether you want just a meeting room for half a day or a complete package for a residential event we can accommodate your requirements. All clients are different so we welcome the opportunity of discussing your particular event.

We have 15 well-appointed bedrooms for residential conference delegates and we have three Meeting Rooms and plenty of break-out areas in the house and in the grounds.

Hurds Hill is the perfect place for a Strategy Retreat. Confidential Board Meeting or Team Event.

Contact: david@hurdshill.com Tel: 07766 572566

www.hurdshill.com

9839176R00022

Printed in Great Britain
by Amazon.co.uk, Ltd.,
Marston Gate.